PROFESSOR PETER COOPER is Professor of Psychology at th
Reading and Honorary NHS Consultant Clinical Psycho.
worked for many years in the field of eating disorders, specializing in
bulimia nervosa and binge-eating. His original book on bulimia nervosa
founded the *Overcoming* series in 1993 and continues to help many thou-
sands of people in the USA, the UK and Europe. The aim of the series is to
help people with a wide range of common problems and disorders to take
control of their own recovery programme using the latest techniques of
cognitive behavioural therapy. Each book, with its specially tailored
programme, is devised by a practising clinician. Many books in the
Overcoming series are now recommended by the UK Department of Health
under the Books on Prescription scheme. Following a self-help programme is recommended as a possible first step for those suffering from
bulimia nervosa by the National Institute for Health and Clinical
Excellence (NICE).

Other titles in the *Overcoming* series:

3-part self-help courses

Overcoming Anxiety Self-Help Course
Overcoming Low Self-Esteem Self-Help Course
Overcoming Panic and Agoraphobia Self-Help Course
Overcoming Social Anxiety and Shyness Self-Help Course

Single-volume books

Overcoming Anger and Irritability
Overcoming Anorexia Nervosa
Overcoming Anxiety
Bulimia Nervosa and Binge-Eating
Overcoming Childhood Trauma
Overcoming Chronic Fatigue
Overcoming Chronic Pain
Overcoming Compulsive Gambling
Overcoming Depression
Overcoming Insomnia and Sleep Problems
Overcoming Low Self-Esteem
Overcoming Mood Swings
Overcoming Obsessive Compulsive Disorder
Overcoming Panic
Overcoming Paranoid and Suspicious Thoughts
Overcoming Problem Drinking
Overcoming Relationship Problems
Overcoming Sexual Problems
Overcoming Social Anxiety and Shyness
Overcoming Traumatic Stress
Overcoming Weight Problems
Overcoming Your Child's Fears and Worries
Overcoming Your Smoking Habit

OVERCOMING BULIMIA AND BINGE EATING SELF-HELP COURSE

A 3-part programme based on
Cognitive Behavioural Techniques

Part Two: Monitoring Your Eating, Setting Up a Meal Plan and Learning How to Prevent Binges

Peter J. Cooper

ROBINSON
London

Constable & Robinson Ltd
3 The Lanchesters
162 Fulham Palace Road
London W6 9ER
www.overcoming.co.uk

First published in the UK by Robinson,
an imprint of Constable & Robinson Ltd 2007

A copy of the British Library Cataloguing in
Publication Data is available from the British Library.

Important Note
This book is not intended as a substitute for medical advice or treatment.
Any person with a condition requiring medical attention should consult
a qualified medical practitioner or suitable therapist.

ISBN: 978-1-84529-236-2 (PACK ISBN)

ISBN: 978-1-84529-506-6 (PART ONE)

ISBN: 978-1-84529-507-3 (PART TWO)

ISBN: 978-1-84529-508-0 (PART THREE)

Printed and bound in the EU

1 3 5 7 9 10 8 6 4 2

Contents

Note to Practitioners

This self-help course is suitable for a wide range of reading abilities and its step-by-step format makes it ideal for working through alone or under supervision. The course is divided into three workbooks, and each contains a full supply of worksheets and charts to be filled in on the page – so there is no need for photocopying. If you do decide to photocopy this material you will need to seek the permission of the publishers to avoid a breach of copyright law.

Introduction: How to Use this Workbook

What's in the workbooks?

This self-help course aims to give people with bulimia nervosa and binge-eating problems a way towards recovery. It is divided into three parts.

Part One explains:

- what bulimia nervosa and binge-eating problems are;
- how they affect people;
- what causes them;
- whether and how you might benefit from the self-help course.

Part Two explains:

- how to set about using the self-help course;
- how to monitor what you eat;
- how to plan your eating;
- how to learn to prevent binges.

Part Three explains:

- how to learn problem-solving skills;
- how to stop dieting;
- how to change how you think;

and also contains a section of useful information.

How long will the course take?

It is not possible to say exactly how long it will take you to work through this self-help course. Different people find different parts easier to manage, and most people hit sticky patches where they need to spend longer working on one task or stage. Don't feel under pressure to move on before you are ready. As a rule of thumb, the whole course usually takes three to six months to complete. But you may need longer than this. Take your time, and go at what feels the right pace for you.

How do I use the books?

These workbooks are just that – books for working in. So feel free to write on them! Don't just fill in the question boxes, worksheets and charts, but make notes in the margins, underline things you think are important, or mark things you don't quite understand and want to come back to. We have provided a few extra pages for your thoughts and reflections at the back of each workbook, should you need extra space.

Will it work for me?

The self-help principles presented in Parts Two and Three of this course are based on cognitive behavioural therapy, a well-tested and proven form of psychological therapy that helps you deal with problems in a very practical and personal way. These principles have been used by many people with bulimia nervosa and binge-eating problems to help them towards recovery. It has been shown in recent research that the great majority of people with bulimia nervosa and binge-eating problems also benefit from these principles when they are accessed via the self-help programme outlined below.

How will I know if I've recovered?

It is important to be clear about what 'recovery' from bulimia nervosa means. Many people do recover fully. They find they can eat normally without anxiety and without the concerns about their weight and shape which used to dominate their lives.

However, many people find they still sometimes have difficulties with food and related concerns, even if these problems only surface on rare occasions of stress. If you find that these difficulties still come up from time to time, this does not mean that you have not recovered. Part of a realistic notion of recovery is accepting that difficulties with eating may occasionally come back, but that they can be dealt with using the principles set out in this course.

Using the book to help someone else

- This book is intended mainly for people who have bulimia nervosa or binge-eating problems themselves. However, it will also be helpful to others. The families and friends of people who binge often want to know more about the problem.

- If you are using the course yourself, it may well be helpful if someone else – a parent, partner or friend – knows what you are trying to do so that they can help and support you.

- Finally, it is suggested in the self-help course that the person using it gets someone to help them. This could be a friend or relative, but it is even better if it is someone less close to them, such as a general practitioner, a nurse or a dietitian. This person will need to know what advice is contained in the course if they are to give the most help they can.

A note on gender

Because most people who binge and/or suffer from bulimia nervosa are women, the user of these books is referred to in the text as 'she' and 'her'. This is by no means intended to imply that the course is directed only at women; some men also suffer from these problems, and they are just as likely to benefit from following this programme.

SECTION 1: Before You Start

How does the self-help course work?

This self-help course doesn't set out to cover everything one could imagine doing that might help people restore their eating habits to normal. Think of it more as a basic toolkit, containing the *essential elements* of a self-help programme. You'll need to fill in much of the specific detail yourself, and this will depend on your own circumstances and what sort of person you are. Used in this way, the course will help many people with bulimia nervosa to deal with their eating problems without specialist help. It is, however, important to state again that for some people this self-help programme may not be enough. If you are among them, it is important that you consult your doctor to get more help.

The course will ask you to follow specific guidelines in a particular order, and you may find this quite demanding. However, these guidelines are known to help people with bulimia nervosa receiving treatment in specialist clinics, and the more closely you follow them, the more likely it is that the course will help you regain control over your eating. So if at first you feel rather overwhelmed by how much you are going to have to do to overcome your problems with eating, do not be too daunted. Remember:

- The course is a gradual process, moving on step by step, and you can set the pace.

- Although the course specifies definite measures you must take in order to recover, *you aren't expected to follow these measures for ever*.

The goal of this course is to get you to the point

- where food is no longer a threat to you;

- where you can eat normally and with enjoyment, and

- without anxieties about your weight and shape.

On the way there, however, you will have to think a great deal about food and eating and about your weight and shape. That is, in order to free yourself from your preoccupation with food, eating, weight and shape, for a while you will need to pay particular attention to your eating and your concerns about weight and shape.

How long it will take to recover varies greatly from individual to individual, as noted in the Introduction. Don't worry at this stage how long it will take for you. However, if you find that you have made a real effort to use the manual and have not been able to make any progress at all in, say, around six weeks, then it would be sensible to stop trying to use it alone and consult your doctor about getting further help. If, on the other hand, you have made even just a little progress, then as long as you continue to progress it is worth persevering.

The six steps

There are six steps to the self-help course, shown in the diagram below.

1: Monitoring your eating

Keeping a regular written record so that you can see exactly what, and when, you have been eating

↓

2: Setting up a meal plan

Deciding what is a sensible pattern of eating, and trying to keep to it

↓

3: Learning what to do to prevent binges

Finding out what kinds of events and feelings cause you to binge, and what you can do to stop this happening

↓

4: Problem solving

Learning how to pinpoint the problems that cause difficulties in your eating, and how to deal with them

↓

5: Stopping dieting

Deliberately and consistently widening the range of foods you eat

↓

6: Changing your mind

Identifying some of the beliefs that lie beneath your difficulties with eating and learning how to challenge them

These steps follow one another in the order given: this workbook, Part Two, covers the first three, and the next one, Part Three, covers steps four to six. Each step has a complete section of the workbook devoted to it, and it's important to tackle them in the order in which they are set out.

At the end of each step there is a box headed 'Before you move on'. This consists of a set of questions for you to ask yourself about the progress you have made. Only when you are able to answer 'yes' to all the questions should you proceed to the next section of the course. If you find yourself answering 'no' to one or more questions, stay with the same section and spend a bit more time working on that step.

How to start working on the course

There is a lot of information in these workbooks. If you read right through the course, then put the books aside and try to follow all the advice at once, you will not succeed.

It is essential that you follow the steps in the order they come and only go on to the next step when you are ready to do so.

Having said that, it is a good idea to read through the whole of Parts Two and Three first to get an overall idea of what they contain. This advice alone might put off some people who have serious difficulties in concentrating. If this is how you feel, don't give up: just spend ten minutes skimming through the workbooks, perhaps just reading the headings and subheadings; this will be enough to give you a rough idea of what is there.

Having read through (or at least skimmed through) Parts Two and Three, you will be ready to begin on Step 1. However, before you do so, read it through again; or, if you didn't read all of it when you were skimming through the whole course, read it all now. You'll need to refer to the workbooks again and again while you're working through the course, so keep handy whichever one you are working on at the moment. And remember, don't try to rush ahead; if you try to follow some particular piece of advice given in the manual and it does not work out as planned, don't give up: just go back to the relevant section, re-read it, and try to work out why things went wrong and what you should do next time to improve your chances of succeeding.

Recruiting a helper

Some people whose eating is not very seriously disturbed will be able to use this course entirely on their own. However, for many people with bulimia nervosa this is an unrealistic expectation. The problem is that, however hard you try to stick to the guidelines set out in these workbooks, there are bound to be times when things do not go well. At these times it is difficult not to become depressed, to blame yourself, and to feel like giving up. Having someone to talk to about what has happened and what you might be able to do about it can be a real help.

You could ask a close friend or relative to be your helper. However, it is usually better to recruit someone who does not have a close relationship with you in your ordinary life, and who can therefore be objective. Your doctor or healthcare provider (in the UK, the practice nurse) is probably a better person to choose than a friend. It is particularly good if you can see your helper regularly. Ideally this should be every week at first, but soon this can be less frequent.

In the 'Useful Information' section at the end of Part Three there is a brief section for helpers setting out how they can best support you as you work through the self-help course. You should show this to the person you ask to help you.

Be prepared for a struggle!

Many people read right through the course and then immediately feel charged up with enthusiasm to tackle their difficulties with eating. Many also feel, the first time something goes wrong, that they have totally failed and will never succeed. It is important to stress that *if overcoming your problems with eating were easy, you would have done it long ago*. It is going to be a struggle, and there will be times when you will not manage to achieve as much as you want to. However, if you are attempting to follow the guidelines set out in this manual, you are making an effort at taking control of your eating; and *any success at all is an improvement on which further improvements can be built*.

It often turns out that at some point, perhaps some months after starting out, suddenly things become much easier and the prospect of a life of 'normal' eating becomes a real possibility. So, even if you are just creeping forward, it is well worth carrying on and waiting for the breakthrough.

Some advice about weight and weight control

Before setting out on the self-help course, it is useful to consider:

- what is an appropriate weight for you;
- what is a sensible, regular system of weighing yourself;

- how constantly checking your body shape can be unhelpful;
- what is an appropriate level of exercise for you to do.

How much should you weigh?

It is hard for anyone to state exactly what is the 'correct' weight for you. Some people argue that your weight should not be allowed to fall more than 15 per cent below the average for your age, height and sex, because below that weight the physiological and psychological effects of starvation will make it virtually impossible for you to eat normally. Others argue that the 'correct' weight is the weight you were before your problems with eating began. Both of these definitions can be helpful in many cases, but neither is entirely satisfactory. Some people whose relatives are all overweight, and whose natural weight is higher than the average, would experience starvation symptoms well before they weighed 15 per cent less than the average. And for many people with bulimia nervosa who have a long history of disturbed eating habits of one sort or another, it is impossible to identify a point at which their eating was sufficiently 'normal' to identify a natural body weight.

The range of appropriate weights is shown in the chart below.

1 Definitely underweight
2 Desirable range for health
3 A little overweight, but not likely to affect health
4 Overweight. Health could be adversely affected
5 Considerably overweight. Definitely at medical risk and in need of treatment

Source: Adapted from *Obesity and Related Diseases* by John Garrow (1988), by kind permission of Elsener.

You might find it helpful to consider what would be a healthy weight for a person of your height. It may also be worth your considering where the weight you would ideally like to be is in relation to the norms shown in the figure. Many people with bulimia nervosa want to be at a very low weight, and if they are going to recover from their eating disorder and manage to eat normally they are going to have to give up this desire to weigh so little and replace it with a more realistic target weight range.

With this in mind, try the following short exercise:

1   What is your height?

_____

2   What weight would you like to be?

Between_____and_____

3   Looking at the chart of weights, what would be a healthy weight for a person of this height?

Between_____and_____

If there is a big gap between what you have written in answer to questions **2** and **3**, you may have to work on changing your expectations of what you should weigh.

'Natural weight' means the weight at which your body would settle if you were eating perfectly normally. It will vary quite a lot from one individual to another. This weight is determined by two things:

- genetic factors (i.e. factors which you have inherited from your parents);

- the balance between how much you eat and how much energy you expend.

There is only one way to discover what your natural weight is, and that is *to reinstate normal eating habits and then see over a period of several months what happens to your weight*.

It is also important to remember that weight does not ordinarily stay fixed at exactly the same point. Rather, it is quite 'normal' for body weight to go up or down by a few pounds over the course of, say, a week. So if you do have in your mind an acceptable weight, this should be a range (with a margin of two or three pounds in either direction) rather than one fixed number. Remember, too, that weight goes up and down naturally over the menstrual cycle. Premenstrual water retention, bloatedness and 'weight gain' are very common and a result of normal hormonal changes.

Most people who follow the principles set out in this self-help course find that their weight does not change significantly. Although some people do lose weight, most never achieve the weight they would ideally like to be. This is because their ideal weight is usually unrealistically low and simply not achievable without starving themselves to a point where they would be at serious medical risk.

The important point for people with bulimia nervosa is that there is often a trade-off to be made between weight and eating habits. Thus, you may well find that, having worked right through this self-help course, you can eat normally but that your weight is, say, a few pounds more than you would like it to be; on the other hand, if you diet and lose those few pounds, then you will not be able to maintain control of your eating and binge-eating will return.

Ultimately the choice here will be entirely yours. Ask yourself:

'Is weighing a few pounds more than I am entirely happy with a worthwhile price to pay for normal eating habits and the kind of life this allows me to lead?'

Or, to put it the other way round:

'Is weighing a few pounds less a worthwhile goal, given that the cost is perpetually disturbed eating habits and the effect they have on the rest of my life?'

It is not worth considering your answer in any detail at this point, because you won't know the exact nature of the choice until you are eating normally and your weight has settled at some point. But if you follow the treatment programme it is likely that you will eventually be faced with these questions.

Some people are very lucky and find that their weight settles exactly where they always wished it to be. Others are less fortunate. For the great majority the outcome is the same as it is for everybody else: their weight is a little above what they would prefer it to be.

The sensible thing to do at this stage, when you are just beginning to try to restore some order to your eating habits, is to postpone any decision about what weight would be acceptable to you until you have regained control of your eating and seen precisely what effect this has actually had on your weight.

Weighing yourself

There are two common ways in which people with bulimia nervosa deal with weighing themselves.

- Some get on and off the scales frequently, to check what effect binge-eating, vomiting, and so on has had on their weight.

- Many others avoid weighing themselves altogether because it distresses them too much.

Many alternate between the two extremes, depending on the degree of control over their eating and whether their weight is high or low.
     Neither solution is satisfactory.

- Frequent weighing merely serves to increase the level of concern and preoccupation with weight by highlighting small and insignificant fluctuations.

- Completely avoiding weighing also increases anxiety about what the weight might really be.

Certainly, changing your eating habits, as you will do if you follow the programme, is likely to have effects on your weight, and if you are to make rational decisions about your behaviour you ought to be aware of exactly what these effects are.

The appropriate solution is to weigh yourself once a week.

- This should be at the same time each week (Friday morning is a good time for many people).

- Given that on some occasions this may be an upsetting experience for you (and when you are upset you are likely to feel like eating), it is wise to choose a time of the day when it is going to be difficult for you to eat (such as just before you have to leave the house for work).

- Record your weight so you can track its progress.

- Make this weekly weighing compulsory: don't skip it, and don't weigh yourself at any other time.

For some people, sticking to this weekly weighing is going to be very difficult.

- If you have avoided weighing yourself for some time you will find it hard to begin. Unfortunately there is no easy way to start: you will simply have to steel yourself. But you will find that once you have started it can become a relatively simple routine.

- On the other hand, if you are weighing yourself frequently at the moment – say, many times a day – it will be very difficult to restrict weighing to once a week. The best way to do it is to put yourself on a programme to cut down the frequency of weighing bit by bit. For example, for the first week you should restrict weighing to once a day. For the second week you should weigh every second day. And so on.

By the end of four weeks you should be on the once-a-week weighing schedule.

Checking body shape

It is common for people with bulimia nervosa to make frequent checks on their body shape, just as they might make frequent checks on their weight.

- They might use a tape measure to judge the 'fatness' of particular parts of their body, such as their thighs or their waist.

- They might inspect themselves regularly in the mirror.

- They might pinch certain parts of themselves (like their stomach) to gauge how 'fat' they are.

- They might judge their body shape by how tight their clothes feel.

Checking your body shape in this way is not a good idea and you should try to stop doing it.

Making these checks simply increases your concerns about your shape. You feel happy when the check produces a desirable result and distressed when the results are unsatisfactory. And the problem is that these responses then come to govern your subsequent actions. Thus, it is common for people who have examined themselves in the mirror and decided that they are fat to immediately go and binge.

It is important, therefore, that you stop making such checks of your body shape. If you find this really hard, you can phase out the checks gradually, in the way described above for people who weigh themselves very often. However, the sooner they are stopped the better.

Judging body shape by how tight clothes feel is particularly unhelpful because some clothes shrink when they are washed; and the result is that you feel fatter when you are wearing clean clothes! If you are in the habit of judging your shape by the feel of your clothes, then it would be a good idea to take all your clothes that are tight (jeans and skirts are especially important) and either alter them so that they fit more loosely or get rid of them. Some people keep in the wardrobe clothes they used to wear some time ago when they were much thinner. Their intention is to start wearing them again when they have successfully reduced their weight. *This is most unhelpful.* It encourages dieting which, in turn, encourages binge-eating. And the small clothes are a depressing reminder that you are not as thin as you would like to be. It would be best if you got rid of them.

Taking the right amount of exercise

Exercise is much encouraged these days because of its positive benefits to health; and many people with bulimia nervosa say that they definitely feel much better about themselves when they are taking regular exercise. However, many people use excessive exercise as a method of compensating for overeating. This is not healthy and serves to perpetuate concerns about food, eating, weight and shape.

If you are using exercise primarily as a means of weight control, you should keep a record of exactly how much time you are spending exercising. You can then review this and adopt a programme of appropriate exercise. You may well find this difficult and so – just as with weighing yourself and checking your body shape – you may need to reduce the amount you exercise in stages. The two key points to remember are:

- You should exercise because you enjoy it and because it is physically good for you.

- Any exercise which is taken principally for weight control reasons or to compensate for overeating is not advisable.

SECTION 2: Monitoring Your Eating

Note: Read through all of this section before you start to put it into action.

Why monitor what you eat?

If you are going to begin trying to change your eating habits, then it is important that you know exactly what is happening with your eating at the moment. For this reason *it is essential that you keep a detailed record every day of*:

- when you eat;
- what you eat;
- where you eat;
- whether you feel that what you ate was excessive;
- whether you feel out of control;
- whether you vomit or take laxatives;
- any other circumstances that might be relevant to reorganizing your eating habits.

At first, keeping such a record might seem both tedious and pointless. It might even seem like a punishment, in that by making you more aware of your eating habits it makes you feel worse. However, if you are to begin to change you have to become aware of exactly what is happening with your eating; and you will soon realize that this record is a key tool in this process.

General guidelines for monitoring

In keeping this record, it will be helpful for you to stick to the following guidelines:

- Use a standard form, like the one on page 13. Several more copies of this form that you can fill in are provided at the end of this workbook.
- Use a separate form (more than one if necessary) for each day.

- Record everything you eat (not just things you feel happy about having eaten), and do not stop monitoring when your eating goes wrong.

- Write down what you have eaten immediately after having done so, rather than trying to remember everything at the end of the day.

Specific guidelines for monitoring

Record when you eat and drink

The first column is for recording the time when food is eaten. Try to be reasonably accurate about this because, as will become clear later, it is important.

Record what you eat and drink

The second column is for recording all the food (and liquid) that you eat and drink during the day. Again, you'll need to be accurate – but not *over*-precise. So:

- As already noted, write this down soon after the episode of eating. This obviously means that you will need to carry the workbook, or a copy of the monitoring sheet, with you at all times.

- Describe what you have eaten but don't weigh or measure it. So, if you eat two chocolate bars, rather than just writing down 'chocolate', record it as, say, 'two Mars bars'; but if you've had a bowl of cereal, don't weigh it out beforehand and write down '100 grams All Bran': 'a small bowl of All Bran' will do. And *you should NOT record the calorie content*.

Since your aim in following this self-help programme is to restore healthy eating habits, it is important that you indicate on your monitoring sheets when you ate a normal meal. It may be difficult for you to decide on what is and what is not a 'normal meal'.

A normal meal is an episode of eating where food is eaten in a controlled and organized manner.

Monitoring Sheet   Date: _____   Day: _____

Time	Food and liquid consumed	Place	B	C	Events/feelings

So, if you

- intended to eat certain food,

- at a certain time; and

- did so in a normal fashion and

- without feeling out of control,

you can regard this as a meal.
   And remember:

- *how much* you eat should not influence whether you decide to call the episode a meal.

Normal meals should be distinguished on your monitoring sheets from all other eating by marking them with a bracket. For an example of how this is done, see the completed example in the next section (page 27).

Record where you eat and drink

The third column on the monitoring sheet is for you to record where the episode of eating took place. Again, you should be fairly precise about this: it is better to say 'the kitchen' than just 'at home'.

Record whether you feel you have eaten too much

The fourth column, headed B, is for recording whether or not you felt the food eaten was excessive. This should be done by placing an asterisk (*) in this column next to any item of food which you felt at the time was excessive and which you wish you had not eaten.
   You may regard eating as excessive for one of two reasons:

- first, because of the *quantity* eaten (e.g. three potatoes when you felt you should have had only one);

- second, because of the *type* of food eaten (e.g. a chocolate bar, when you felt you should not have eaten chocolate).

It is important that all food eaten in a binge is recorded on the monitoring sheet; in these cases, each item will be marked with an asterisk.

Record whether and how you have tried to compensate for overeating

The fifth column (headed C) is for recording your attempts to compensate for overeating by

- vomiting;

- taking laxatives or diuretics, and/or

- exercising.

You can show which particular way of compensating you have used by writing down the initial letter: so, for instance, in the completed example on page 17 'V' means 'vomited' and 'L' means 'used laxatives'.

Record how you feel

The sixth and final column is for recording how you feel at the time you eat anything, particularly after episodes of overeating but also when you have a planned meal or snack (as described in Section 3 on 'Setting Up a Meal Plan').

You might record here:

- feelings prompted by everyday events of life, such as having a minor argument with a friend or parent;

- feelings prompted by an event concerned specifically with eating, such as having been obliged by social pressure to eat something with which you were not happy;

- feelings of unhappiness, anger, anxiety, boredom or frustration – whether related to your eating problem, to your concerns about your weight or shape, or to other aspects of your life.

This column is especially significant because, if you have overeaten, it is important that you try to pinpoint for yourself

- what the circumstances were in which this episode occurred, and

- what you were feeling and thinking at the time.

By doing this you will come to understand in detail what sorts of things lead you to binge. That knowledge is itself a big step towards learning how to intervene to prevent binges, as we shall see in Section 4 of this workbook.

This column should also be used for recording when you weigh yourself (and how much you weigh). If you check your shape, you should record this here as well so you can get a good idea of how often this happens and what effect it has on you.

An example of how to use the monitoring sheets

The sample monitoring sheet shown opposite is a real account of one person's eating during one day.

You will see that her day – a Monday – began badly because she weighed herself and discovered that her weight had increased by three pounds over the previous weekend. In the light of this discovery she resolved not to eat at all that day.

She managed not to eat until 1.30 p.m., when she had an apple. She regretted this (indicated by the asterisk) because she feared that to eat anything at all raised the chances of her losing control later. In fact she managed to avoid eating anything else until 5.15 p.m.

At this point, having felt terribly hungry all afternoon, her resolve weakened and she had a bar of chocolate. She deeply regretted this; then she completely lost control and had a full-blown binge (all items marked with an asterisk), after which she immediately made herself sick (indicated on the monitoring sheet with the letter V).

She was determined not to eat anything further that day, but at nine o'clock she gave way to the powerful urge to eat and had another binge which was followed again by vomiting (twice). She also took 10 laxative tablets (indicated on the monitoring sheet with the letter L). She was terribly upset by the loss of control and was very much afraid that her weight had gone up even more as a result.

Using fresh monitoring sheets

Seven blank monitoring sheets are provided at the end of this workbook. Use these to record all the food you eat over the next week. In this way you can refer directly to the principles you are supposed to be following, outlined in the preceding pages. Having used these pages, for the weeks to come you can make up your own monitoring sheets in a separate booklet. Be sure to keep all your completed monitoring sheets as a record of your progress.

Monitoring Sheet   Date: 6th June   Day: Monday

Time	Food and liquid consumed	Place	B	C	Events/feelings
8.30	Black coffee x 2	Kitchen			Weight: 8st 3lbs Weight up 3 lbs after a terrible weekend I must not eat today
10.30	Black coffee	Snack bar			
12.00	Black coffee	College			
1.00	Black coffee	College			
1.30	Apple	College	*		Feel so hungry, very tempted to binge. Made myself go back to the library.
3.00	Tea	Snack bar			Hungry
4.00	Tea	Snack bar			
5.15	Small bar of whole nut chocolate	On way home	*		Walking home, couldn't stop myself from buying chocolate.
5.20	Mars bar x 1, Snickers bar x 1	On way home	*		
5.30	Hamburgers x 2 Bag of chips x 2 Bagel x 1	On way home	*		Then went from shop to shop eating all the way home.
5.45	6 doughnuts	Kitchen	*	V	Feel disgusted with myself. No more food allowed today.
6.15	Cup of tea	Kitchen		V	
8.00	Cup of coffee	My room		V	
9.00	Slice of toast (dry)	Kitchen	*		Help! I can't stop eating
9.05	Slice of toast and cheese	Kitchen	*		I hate myself. I'm going to get fatter and fatter.
"	6 slices of toast and cheese/jam	"	*		
9.20	Bowl of cereal x 2	Kitchen	*		I wish I was dead
9.40	4 slices of toast and butter	Kitchen	*	V	
10.15	Cup of tea	Kitchen		L	I will not eat tomorrow.

Reviewing your monitoring sheets

Once you have been monitoring your eating for a week, review the week as a whole and start trying to identify any patterns in your eating. This reviewing process will continue throughout the self-help programme and will provide valuable information for you to use in deciding which techniques and methods will be helpful to you in regaining control of your eating. The sample review sheet opposite shows the kinds of questions you should ask yourself at this stage. There is space at the bottom of the sheet for you to add any other comments about how you feel about the week's efforts.

If you fill in one of these review sheets every week, you will gradually come to a clearer understanding of the nature of your eating problem, which is crucial to your further attempts to stop binge-eating and restore your eating habits to 'normal'. (More blank sheets are provided at the end of this workbook.)

It is particularly important at this stage to begin to identify times and situations when you are especially vulnerable to binge-eating. Advice on how to deal with these situations is presented in Sections 3 and 4.

You should make a fixed appointment with yourself each week to review your monitoring sheets, record what you can learn from them in a fresh review sheet, and make definite goals for the next week.

If you are seeing a helper, it is useful to take along the results of these review sessions.

Review of this week's monitoring

Week from_____to_____

What are the particular times when binges seem more likely to occur?

_____

_____

What are the particular situations which tend to trigger binges?

_____

_____

Are there times when eating is relatively easy to control?

_____

_____

What types of food have you been eating during binges?

_____

_____

Are these foods different from the types you eat at other times, and if so how?

_____

_____

Are there long periods of time when you eat nothing at all?   YES / NO

How many times this week has a period of eating nothing
at all been followed by a binge?   _____

How many times this week has a day of strict dieting been
followed by a day when you binge?   _____

Any other observations

_____

_____

Before you move on

Before moving on to the next step of the course in Section 3, ask yourself the following questions:

Am I writing down everything I eat on my monitoring sheets?	YES / NO
Does this include everything I eat in binges?	YES / NO
Am I doing this soon after having eaten?	YES / NO
Am I keeping these records systematically (that is, using a standard system of recording on standard forms)?	YES / NO
Am I reviewing my monitoring sheets regularly to try to identify patterns in my eating habits?	YES / NO

If you can answer 'yes' to all these questions, go on to Section 3. If you cannot answer 'yes' to all the questions, you should re-read Section 2 and try again to follow all the guidelines it contains for another week or so. Then ask yourself these questions again. Do not be tempted to move on until you are confident you are monitoring your eating following the guidelines set out in this section.

SECTION 3: Setting Up a Meal Plan

Note: Read through all of this section before you start to put it into action.

The next stage of the programme involves learning to eat regularly and in a controlled fashion. More specifically, it means that from now on *you must eat three meals and two or three snacks a day*.

Many people will see this as a recipe for disaster. They will be saying to themselves: 'If I abandon my efforts to diet and start eating meals and snacks I will gain weight and inevitably get fat.' Well, of course, this would be perfectly correct if you ate meals and snacks and continued, in addition, to binge. But the meal plan is intended to displace the binges, so that you will almost certainly be eating less overall than you were before.

It is definitely not the case that by eating regular meals you will become fat.

Why have a meal plan?

The key idea in setting up a meal plan is to decide in advance exactly when you are going to eat, *irrespective of whether or not you feel like eating when that time comes*. It is important at this stage that you eat according to a predetermined plan, and not according to when you feel hungry. At this early stage, *you cannot trust your sensations of hunger or fullness and they should be ignored*.

You will also have to decide what sorts of food you should eat and in what quantity.

Deciding when to eat

Setting down in advance the times when you will eat has a number of benefits. In particular,

- it permits or legitimizes eating at certain times; and
- it makes it explicit that at other times you are not supposed to be eating.

Once you have decided on an eating pattern it is very important that you make every effort to stick to it.

...t for eating, you must eat, even if you do not feel hungry ...nage to go a few more hours without eating.

...e times set for eating, you must try your hardest not

...place the pattern of alternating between not eating at all for ...reating with a pattern of regular eating.

...n of pre-set regular eating is to work, there should rarely be a gap of longer ...three or four hours between set times for eating. This means that the meal plan must consist of three meals a day and two or three snacks.

It is important to repeat that once you have decided on a plan, the specified meals and snacks are not optional but obligatory; that is, *you must eat when you have planned to do so, and you must try not to eat when you have not planned to do so.*

A sample meal plan

The following is an example of what would constitute a sensible meal plan:

7.30 a.m.	Breakfast
10.00 a.m.	Snack
1.00 p.m.	Lunch
4.30 p.m.	Snack
7.30 p.m.	Supper
10.30 p.m.	Snack

You may well be alarmed by this example because it includes so many times for eating. However, it is important that your meal plan is not very different from this one. The reason for this is that *such a plan is effective at displacing binge-eating precisely because the gaps of time between episodes of planned eating are quite short*. What this means is that if ever you feel like eating when you are not supposed to, you can reassure yourself with the knowledge that it is not long until you will have a meal or snack.

Now write out in the space below a meal plan of your own, using the one above as a model. You might need to make the times slightly different to fit your own routine – for example, when you have to have breakfast to get to work, or to make your meals fit with family commitments – but remember not to leave more than three or four hours between any two 'eating times'.

_____ a.m.   Breakfast

_____ a.m.   Snack

_____ p.m.   Lunch

_____ p.m.   Snack

_____ p.m.   Supper

_____ p.m.   Snack

Alternative meal plans

Clearly, the exact times of these meals and snacks must be tailored to your own particular circumstances; and it is probably wise to have a special plan for weekends, holidays and other times when your usual daily routine does not apply. Try filling in another one here that would suit your usual weekend routine:

_____ a.m.   Breakfast

_____ a.m.   Snack

_____ p.m.   Lunch

_____ p.m.   Snack

_____ p.m.   Supper

_____ p.m.   Snack

There may be other times at which you need a different plan – for example, if you have children, in the school holidays; or if you work shifts, for different times of shifts. There are more blank plans at the back of this workbook if you need them. You will need to cover all the different possibilities. But remember: however you change the times, *there should never be more than three or four hours between one snack or meal and the next.*

If you have children you will need to decide whether to eat with them or to eat separately. For some people, the children's mealtime routine can provide a useful structure on which to map their own meal plans. For others, children's meals represent a major problem as a time when there is a lot of food around which they find difficult not to eat. Leftovers can be a particular problem. You must decide in advance which system is going to make it easier for you to stick to your meal plan, and set your times to fit that decision.

It's worth repeating the key point again:

Each of the meals and snacks specified in these plans represents a time when you must eat.

The meal plan can now be added to your monitoring sheets, so that as you start on this new step of the programme you continue to monitor your eating at the same time. On page 26 is a new version of the monitoring sheet with a section for you to fill in your meal plan. (There are extra blank copies at the end of this workbook.)

Monitoring with meal plans

As you continue monitoring, each time one of your planned mealtimes comes up and you eat something in a controlled and organized fashion, you will indicate this on the sheet with a bracket.

It is important that you stick closely to the times specified on your meal plan and do not eat before a meal or snack is scheduled; and, similarly, it is important that you do not postpone or skip a meal or snack.

A typical monitoring sheet of someone who has established a meal plan (and is doing rather well) is shown on page 27.

Deciding what to eat

It does not matter much at this stage what you eat in your meals and snacks, as long as it is food you feel comfortable with: that is,

- food you can eat without it leading to a binge, and

- food you can eat without having to vomit or take laxatives.

This almost certainly means that it will be low-calorie food, probably diet food. This is not necessarily a problem at this stage, provided you are getting enough to eat. Most people with bulimia nervosa who begin a meal plan do restrict their eating to low-calorie food and eat rather little. The trouble with this, particularly if you are rather thin, is that if you are eating less than your body needs – that is, starving – you will eventually be unable to stick to your meal plan. Thus, if, for example, for every meal or snack you ate a single apple, you would simply not be getting enough to eat; so at some point in the day your control would break down and you would binge. It is, therefore, important, as already noted, that you get enough to eat.

What is 'enough', then? This is likely to be a problem for many people. There are three ways of dealing with it:

- The first is a simple matter of noticing what is happening to your eating. For example, if you are trying to stick to a programme of three meals and three snacks a day, and you find that an hour or so after your lunchtime meal you feel like a binge, then it might be the case that your lunches are too small, leaving you physiologically deprived. If you try increasing the amount you eat for lunch, you will probably not feel hungry before the next scheduled snack and so will be less likely to lose control and binge.

- A second strategy is to use someone else as a reference point. That is, choose a friend or relative who you feel is a 'normal' eater, and take note of how much she eats in a meal. This might help you get an idea of the kind of size to aim at in your own meals.

- The third strategy is to buy some (non-diet) prepared meals for one from a supermarket as a guideline to how much food a meal should contain.

You might also find it helpful, in deciding how much to eat, to talk the problem over with a trusted friend or relative (see the section on 'Talking to someone' in Section 4 below, page 39). Or you could discuss it with your helper.

Don't worry too much if you find it quite hard to decide what foods to include in your meal plan. Many people do at this stage. The important point here is to *try to eat only what you are comfortable with*. In particular you should avoid eating anything which you know will be likely to trigger a binge. This may well mean that you are the only person not having a second helping or not having a dessert. This can be embarrassing, but at least you will have the satisfaction of knowing that you have stuck to your meal plan and not gone on to binge.

Monitoring sheet with meal plan

Meal Plan   **Date:**   **Day:**

_____ a.m.	Breakfast	_____ p.m.	Snack
_____ a.m.	Snack	_____ p.m.	Supper
_____ p.m.	Lunch	_____ p.m.	Snack

Time	Food and liquid consumed	Place	B	C	Events/feelings

Monitoring sheet with meal plan

Meal Plan   **Date:** 21st September   **Day:** Wednesday

Breakfast: Egg/toast   Snack: Crunchy bar

Snack: Apple   Supper: Fish, baked potato, peas, orange

Lunch: Cheese sandwich and yogurt   Snack: Apple

Time	Food and liquid consumed	Place	B	C	Context of /feelings
7.45	Boiled egg, 2 slices of toast Low fat spread Cup of tea x 2	Kitchen			Egg and toast – felt like a lot to eat in one go.
10.30	Apple Coffee	Office			Not hungry but made myself have this.
1.00	2 slices of bread Low fat cream cheese Cucumber V. low fat strawberry yogurt	Park	*		I feel guilty, all that bread. Feel like I'm going to gain weight.
1.45	Cup of tea	Office			
4.00	Cereal bar (apricot and nut) Cup of tea	Office Kitchen			Break a bit earlier than usual. Feel self conscious, no one else is eating.
7.30	Fish in parsley sauce Baked potato, peas Orange Coffee	Kitchen			Ate the same as the rest of the family for the first time in ages – had a smaller portion.
10.30	Cup of tea Apple	Lounge			This is a dangerous time. I'm going straight to bed. I'm <u>not</u> going to get up.

Planning what to eat in advance

Deciding what to eat can be a problem, particularly when you are feeling hungry. *It is a good idea, therefore, to plan in advance what you are going to eat*. Some people find that this is best done immediately before a meal or snack; others find it helpful to sketch out a plan before going to bed at night. A good method, which takes what you have already been doing one step further, is to fill in *what* you are going to eat as well as *when* you are going to eat it at the top of your monitoring sheet for the next day's eating. On the opposite page is an example of a monitoring sheet prepared in this way on a Monday evening for the next day.

If you do this, you will then be able to check if you are keeping to your plan as you fill in the sheet throughout the day. If you find it hard to state exactly what you will have for each meal or snack, you could just note a few limited alternatives. You will have to find out for yourself whether planning immediately before a meal or a day in advance is best for you.

Some useful strategies for making and keeping a meal plan

Ending a meal with a 'full stop'

It is useful to remove all decisions about your eating from the actual time when you are eating.

Planning meals and snacks ahead of time is one way of doing this. Another is to decide before you begin a meal exactly how much you are going to have. This can be helpful because otherwise it is easy to find that you have eaten more than you are happy with and then feel that you might as well go on and binge. A useful way to do this is to set out your meal or snack and decide that one item (say, a piece of fruit) will be the 'full stop' to the meal. When you have eaten the 'full stop', the meal is over.

Follow the plan, not your feelings

It is essential that you stick to the decisions that you have made in advance.

If, having eaten your 'full stop', you think that you still feel hungry, you must try to ignore this feeling and stick to your decision not to eat any more. The reason for this is that your feelings of hunger or fullness at this stage are unreliable, and if you let them divert you away from your eating plan your eating will soon become disorganized again.

Monitoring sheet with meal plan, including content of meal and snacks

Meal Plan   **Date:** 9th June   **Day:** Tuesday

7.30am Breakfast: Toast and marmalade, orange

10.00am Snack: Banana

1.00pm Lunch: Tuna sandwich and yogurt

4.30pm Snack: Oaty biscuit

7.00pm Supper: Grilled chicken, rice, green salad and apple

10.30pm Snack: Dried fruit

Time	Food and liquid consumed	Place	B	C	Context of /feelings

Making changes to the plan in a controlled way

You may find that the plan you devised in advance wasn't quite right and needs to be changed here and there. It is generally unwise to make changes in the course of the day. A much better idea is to make a new plan for the following day having learned from the mistakes of today.

So, as you fill in your monitoring sheet each day, remember to note in the last column any difficulties you had sticking to your plan; then, when you review it at the end of the day, see what you can learn from it about the particular meal plan you devised. This can help you improve the plan for the next day.

Introducing a meal plan in stages

For a few people, who are fasting for long periods or who binge repeatedly throughout the day, the idea of setting up a meal plan for the entire day is too daunting a prospect. If this is the case for you, divide the day up into three or four chunks of time and begin by setting up an eating plan just for the easiest chunk. Once order is restored to this part of the day and you are able to stick to a plan for those few hours, you can then concentrate on the next least difficult part of the day, and so on.

Dealing with problems

Once you decide on an appropriate meal plan for you, do not assume that you will be able to stick to it straight away. You are almost certain to run into difficulties. The aim at this stage is for you to begin gradually to increase the gaps between these times of difficulty, so that binge-eating becomes less and less frequent and normal meals and snacks become more and more the norm.

Remember, by examining your monitoring sheet at the end of each day, even if things have not gone according to plan, you can learn from your mistakes and make changes to your future plans.

Whatever has happened on a particular day, it is essential that you begin the following day afresh, committed to your meal plan for that day.

Dealing with times when things go wrong

If you run into difficulties during the day, you will probably feel tempted to abandon all effort to keep to your plan for the rest of that day. For example, you may be offered a piece of cake, eat it (when you should not have done so because it was not planned) and then go on to binge; and then immediately resolve not to eat at all for the rest of the day to compensate for having overeaten. This is a grave mistake and will almost certainly lead to further overeating.

The important thing to do when something goes wrong is to get yourself back on your plan as soon as possible.

So, if you ate that piece of cake at five o'clock, the right thing to do would have been to resolve to eat the meal planned for supper. This may seem silly when you have just overeaten, but getting back on to the plan is your only real protection against further episodes of loss of control.

Of course, this is going to be extremely difficult, and when you have overeaten the temptation to diet or fast is likely to be very strong. *But you must fight this temptation and overcome it*. If you give in and cut back on your eating, you will be going completely against the point of the meal plan. The most you should allow yourself to do is to sit down in advance of the meal with your meal plan and replace certain filling items (like a sandwich or baked potato) with lighter, less filling food (like fruit or yogurt). Even this process of making substitutions in your meal plan can be dangerous, because the urge not to eat at all could be very strong and you may be tempted to replace the entire meal with, say, a few grapes. This will not work. The important thing here is to have the meal and for that meal to be a genuine one.

It is often very difficult to follow this advice, especially after a full-blown binge. At such times you are likely to feel disgusted and ashamed with yourself, and to feel particularly acutely the loneliness of trying to sort your problems out on your own. So it is important that you find a way of picking yourself up and carrying on, however difficult this is and however low you feel. It might be helpful at such times to ask yourself: *'Have I made any progress at all? Because if I have, then, however bad I feel at this moment, it is this progress which is really important.'* This is another reason why it is important to keep all your monitoring sheets, and get used to looking out, when you review them, for every little sign of progress you make.

If you ask yourself this question and, after several weeks of trying, can honestly answer, 'No, I really haven't made any progress at all,' then it is time to accept that you need more help, and you should go to see your doctor.

It is inevitable that there will be slip-ups during the time you are working towards recovery. And they will make you very unhappy; at times, they might make you feel hopeless about ever really changing. But, *if you do not allow these slip-ups to overwhelm you, it is possible to learn from them and to move forward*. It can be particularly useful to discuss these slip-ups with a helper, and to talk about your reaction to them, and how you can learn from them.

Dealing with disruptions

There will be occasions when, through no fault of your own, your plans for the day are disrupted. For example, just before you sit down to have lunch, a friend arrives and insists that you accompany her to a restaurant. The way to cope with this is to accept that, from time to time, your plan will have to be revised in the light of unexpected events. Try not to panic when this happens, but instead take a moment to yourself to make changes to your plan for the rest of the day on the basis of the new developments. In general, you should try to change as little as possible, so that the revised plan remains close to your original plan.

Below is an example of one person's meal plan threatened by an unforeseen event, showing how the person coped with the disruption by revising their plan.

Original meal plan

Meal Plan	**Date:** 14th September	**Day:** Wednesday
7.30am	Breakfast:	Poached egg on toast
10.00am	Snack:	Apple
1.00pm	Lunch:	Cottage cheese salad and two crispbreads with low-fat spread Banana
4.30pm	Snack:	Crunchy bar
7.00pm	Supper:	Baked potato with tuna, broccoli
10.30pm	Snack:	Apple

Unexpected event: At 12.45 a friend arrives with news that she has just been offered a new job and insists on going out for lunch to celebrate.

Revised meal plan for the rest of the day

1.00pm	Lunch:	Salad from restaurant menu Person chooses avocado and chicken
		Low-fat dessert from menu Person chooses fruit salad
4.30pm	Snack:	Apple
7.00pm	Supper:	Baked potato with tuna, broccoli Yoghurt
10.30pm	Snack:	Banana

Dealing with special occasions

We have already noted, in the section on 'Alternative meal plans' (page 23), that there will be times when your usual meal plan has to be changed to take circumstances into account. As well as these more regular differences, such as weekends, school holidays and different working shifts, there will be 'one-off' special occasions when you will not be able to stick to your usual plan. You may be obliged to go to a wedding reception, or you may be taken out to dinner by friends or parents, and so on. Here again, although your normal plan will not be appropriate, it is essential that you do have some plan for that particular day, and that the plan is as close to your usual meal plan as possible.

The safest strategy for dealing with a special evening occasion might seem to be to fast throughout the day. This is not a good idea. If you do this, you will be hungry by the evening and much more likely to overeat and then binge.

A far better strategy for an evening special occasion is to alter your routine only slightly, for example:

- Eat as usual until the special evening meal.

- At the meal, have only a starter and a main course (choosing light food with which you will feel comfortable), and no dessert.

- Skip the late evening snack (given that the meal is likely to go on for rather a long time).

Here is another example from the same person's records of how they adjusted their meal plan for their father's birthday dinner:

Usual meal plan for a weekend day		
7.30am	Breakfast:	Bran flakes, banana and milk
10.00am	Snack:	Apple
1.00pm	Lunch:	Scrambled egg on toast Yoghurt
4.30pm	Snack:	Apple
7.00pm	Supper:	Wholewheat pasta with tomato sauce; green salad Banana
10.30pm	Snack:	Two crispbread with low-fat spread

Revised meal plan for the birthday

7.30am	Breakfast:	Bran flakes, banana and milk
10.00am	Snack:	Apple
1.00pm	Lunch:	Scrambled egg on toast Yoghurt
5.00pm	Snack:	Apple
8.00pm	Dinner:	Melon Grilled chicken with new potatoes and tomato salad Coffee

It is essential that you *do not attempt to eat less the following day because of the previous evening's meal*; you should immediately return to your normal meal plan. If you try to compensate for the special meal by eating less, it is very likely that at some point in the day you will binge. It is worth remembering that *no one meal can have a significant effect on your weight*.

Dealing with vomiting

The purpose of establishing a meal plan is to displace binge-eating with 'normal' eating. If you don't binge, you won't feel the need to vomit. So most people will find that, as they get better at eating normally and have fewer binges, there will be correspondingly fewer times when they feel they have to make themselves sick. For this reason, there is often no need to make any special effort to try to stop vomiting.

There are two exceptions to this.

1 Some people find that occasionally, even when they have stuck to their meal plan and eaten exactly what they planned to eat, they feel full, perhaps even bloated, and they become anxious that if they don't vomit they will become fat.

If this happens you must try to resist the urge to vomit. Remember: *vomiting encourages overeating and will therefore work against your efforts to stop binge-eating*. Instead, try to distract yourself until the urge to vomit has passed.

The first time you do this it may take some time for the urge to pass; but, if you do resist this urge, the next time it arises it will pass more quickly, and after a while the urge will disappear altogether.

Experiment with what sorts of distractions work best for you. Most people find that activities like reading or listening to music are not helpful. In fact, apart from going for a walk, which some people do find helpful, solitary activities are probably best avoided. Being with people can have a calming effect and also makes it difficult to escape to vomit.

In the box below, jot down a few ideas of ways you might be able to distract yourself. A couple of suggestions have been included to get you started; obviously, what is appropriate for you will depend on your circumstances.

Distractions from the urge to vomit

Ring a friend for a chat

Go for a walk

Go to the library to choose some books

_____

_____

_____

_____

_____

---

2 The second exception concerns those people who get into the habit of vomiting not only after a binge, but after eating anything at all.

If this is what you do it is essential that, in addition to establishing a meal plan, you work towards eliminating vomiting altogether. Some people can manage this by simply saying to themselves: 'I shall only include in my planned meals and snacks the sort of food I am prepared not to vomit, in the sort of quantities I am prepared to hold down.'

Other people find achieving this end more difficult, and if you are one of them you will have to proceed more gradually.

- Divide the day up into six chunks of time (early morning, late morning, early after-noon, late afternoon, early evening, late evening).

- Ask yourself during which of these would it be easiest (or least difficult) to eat the planned meal or snack without vomiting.

- Once you have made this decision, you should eat without vomiting during this time.

- Use the same sort of distractions as those described above for coping when you have eaten.

- Once you can eat regularly without vomiting during this chunk of time, decide which is the next easiest time and eat the planned meal or snack without vomiting during this time (as well as during the time you have already eliminated vomiting).

In this way vomiting should be gradually eliminated altogether.

Preoccupation with food

Many people who are putting a lot of effort into planning ahead and trying to stick to a meal plan complain that they are having to think about food and eating even more than they did when their eating was completely out of control. In a sense, they say, the treatment is making them feel worse!

This can be distressing, but don't let it worry you too much, because it is a phase which passes in a few weeks. It is just that, if your eating habits have become very disorganized and you are going to restore them to normal, for a while eating will have to occupy a particularly important place in your life. It won't always be like that.

Preoccupation with weight and shape

Many people who begin eating according to a meal plan of the sort described above also find that they become increasingly concerned about their weight and their shape. They are convinced that they are gaining weight and they feel fat.

This is an understandable reaction in someone who has previously been attempt-ing to eat very little. However, if you find that you react in this way, it is important to remember that it is *a psychological reaction to the change in your eating habits rather than a genuine signal of what is happening to your weight and shape*. You will regularly be checking your weight, so you will be able to confirm that replacing binges with regular meals and snacks is not in fact causing you to gain weight or become fat.

These concerns and preoccupations will gradually diminish as you become more confident of your control over eating.

What is a 'good day'?

It is important to be clear about what constitutes a 'good day'.

A 'good day' is one in which you have been able to stick to your meal plan.

Until now you may well have seen as a 'good day' one in which you have been able to avoid eating altogether or, perhaps, managed not to overeat. However, once you establish a meal plan, this is no longer so. You may have a constant struggle throughout an entire day fighting urges to binge when you were not supposed to be eating, forcing yourself to eat planned meals when you desperately wanted to fast, and resisting the urge to vomit; and at the end of such a day you may feel exhausted and demoralized. However, if, despite the great struggle, you were able to stick to your meal plan, eat what you were supposed to eat at the scheduled times, and avoid eating in between scheduled times, then that day was a 'good day' – a personal triumph, in fact. And the more such 'good days' you have, the easier sticking to the meal plan will become.

It is also important to note that if you have one or two slip-ups during a particular day, this does not mean that the day has been 'ruined', and you will need to learn not to see it in this way. If you regard an unscheduled bar of chocolate, for example, as a total disaster, you might be tempted to abandon your attempts at control altogether, feeling that the day has already become a 'bad day', so you might as well binge and start afresh the next day. *This is a very common trap and one which you must avoid.*

If you find that you tend to think in terms of whole days that are either 'good days' or 'bad days', try thinking instead of each day as being divided into smaller chunks of time. Thus, the period between breakfast and the morning snack could be regarded as one chunk, that between the morning snack and lunch as a second chunk, and so on. Each chunk during which you manage to keep control can then be viewed as a separate achievement. If you slip up during, say, the early afternoon you will have 'spoiled' only one of the six or so chunks of the day; and if you can then return immediately to your plan for the rest of the day, as advised, you will still have had five 'good' chunks out of six, which is certainly not a 'bad day'.

Before you move on

Before moving on to the next step of the course in Section 4, ask yourself the following questions:

Have I decided on a meal plan; that is, on definite times when I should eat meals and snacks?	YES / NO
Have I been planning what to eat at these times?	YES / NO
Have I been making sensible modifications to my meal plan to deal with special situations (e.g. holidays, weekends)?	YES / NO
Have I tried to stick to my meal plan every day (even if I haven't ever completely succeeded)?	YES / NO
Have I been trying to get back to my meal plan when things have gone wrong?	YES / NO
Have I attempted not to vomit after eating my planned meals and snacks?	YES / NO

If you can answer *'yes'* to all these questions, you should move on to Section 4. If you cannot answer *'yes'* to all the questions, you should re-read this section and try again to follow all the guidelines it contains.

SECTION 4: Learning What to Do to Prevent Binges

Note: Read through all of this section before you start to put it into action.

If you are trying to stick to a meal plan you have already gone some way towards replacing binge-eating with 'normal' eating habits. However, it is likely that there will be times when you find it very hard to stick to this plan; and it is also likely that there will be times when you have a powerful urge to binge. It is essential that you develop strategies for dealing with these difficulties. The more closely you are able to keep to your meal plan, the less likely you are to binge; so this section suggests some ways to help you both in your efforts to stick to your meal plan and in your attempts to resist the urge to binge.

Talking to someone

Setting up a meal plan and trying to stick to it can be a really daunting task. It is asking a very great deal of yourself to expect to be able to manage this entirely on your own, even with the assistance of a detached helper whom you consult for advice and support.

It can be enormously helpful to enlist the assistance of a close friend or relative as well.

This is not because they can take control and make all the decisions. No one can take over this task and do it for you. But they can help by providing you with certain kinds of very practical assistance. For example:

- It can be a great help to arrange to have some of your evening meals with someone else and to spend time with them afterwards.

- Also, if you know that it is going to be difficult for you to resist eating at a particular time (when you are not supposed to eat), it can be helpful to arrange to spend that time with someone else.

- Similarly, if you can drop in on someone or telephone them when you are feeling particularly like binge-eating, this can see you through the 'crisis' time until the urge fades.

Now, of course, you could make arrangements to do these things without confiding the real reason why you are seeking companionship. However, the secrecy and deceit that loom so large in the lives of people who binge are themselves a great burden and cause much misery. It can be a great relief to tell someone of your troubles, to have someone with whom you don't have to keep up the constant pretence that everything is fine. Also, someone who knows of your particular difficulties can be much more help to you than someone who does not.

You may well feel very nervous about telling anyone about your problems with eating, fearing that they will not understand and will think poorly of you. If you choose someone you respect and trust, this really is most unlikely. It is a sad fact that almost all women within our culture are concerned about their weight and shape, and a great many have problems of some kind with eating. It is not at all difficult for them to see how such problems can become more serious. Almost invariably, the person approached as a confidant will be anxious to be as helpful as they can.

If this is hard for you to accept, think of a good friend and ask yourself how you would react if she came to you in distress and confided some personal difficulty (say, that she was secretly drinking excessively or was shoplifting). How would you react? Surely it is reasonable for you to expect as much acceptance and sympathy as you would be prepared to give.

It is important to stress that the assistance such a friend or relative can provide you with is quite different from the help you could get from an outsider whom you consult as an independent helper.

Planning ahead

However strong your resolve, and however much forethought you put into it, it is not easy to stick to a meal plan. Many things can happen during a day to disrupt your plan, and sometimes you will just feel unable to stick to your good intentions. It is very common for people who binge to think that once something goes wrong with their eating there is nothing they can do to prevent things going rapidly downhill into an inevitable binge. In fact, there is a great deal that you can do to stop things getting worse, at all stages in the process. As with the meal plan itself, a great deal can be achieved by thinking out things in advance:

- spending time planning ahead;

- spotting potential hazards and taking some form of evasive action;

- recognizing the urge to binge early in the process and having a plan for what to do about it.

And, though it may be hard to believe at this stage, it is even possible to stop a binge once you have started.

Some helpful tactics

Here are some of the main things you can do now to make it easier to stick to a meal plan and fend off the urge to binge.

1 *Restrict eating to one or two specified areas within the house.*

These might be, for example, the kitchen and the dining room.

- Make the areas where you usually binge (typically some private space, such as the bedroom) places where food is never allowed.

- If you usually binge in the kitchen, find somewhere else to eat and make it a rule never to eat anything at all in the kitchen.

- If you find it impossible not to 'pick' at food while you cook, keep some chewing gum handy in the kitchen and, when you feel like picking, chew gum instead.

- If you only have one room available to you – a bedsit, perhaps, or a student room – then pinpoint one particular area for eating meals and snacks (such as a particular chair or place at table) and eat there and nowhere else.

Write down here the places where you will eat:

_____

_____

_____

and the places where you will definitely *not* eat:

_____

_____

_____

2 *When you do eat, eat slowly and don't do anything else at the same time.*

Try not to rush your food. This will be easier if you don't eat while, say, reading or watching television.

3 *Before eating a meal, plan exactly what you will do when the meal is finished.*

You might decide, for example, to go for a walk, or make a phone call, or do a household job that will keep your hands occupied. Here is space for you to write down a list of things you could do after meals, so that you can pick one before every meal:

_____

_____

_____

_____

_____

_____

_____

4 *Restrict your supplies of food.*

Buy food in small quantities so that large amounts of food are not easily to hand at home.

5 *Plan your food shopping carefully.*

- Have a list of what you are going to buy.

- Do not shop for food when you feel hungry or think that you are likely to binge.

- If shopping is a particularly difficult time for you, arrange to shop with someone else.

- When you are planning to shop for particular items, take only just enough money and don't carry debit or credit cards.

6 *Don't leave leftover food lying around.*

In fact, it is far better to throw leftovers away than to leave them around where they can threaten your control over your eating. This may feel wasteful and wrong; but it is better to be wasteful temporarily as a way of helping yourself recover than to avoid wasting anything and thereby make it impossible for you to stop binge-eating. And think of it this way: isn't binge-eating and then vomiting much *more* wasteful than throwing away a few uneaten bits of a family meal?

7 *Don't allow anyone to bully you into eating anything you do not want.*

You may well find people trying to press food upon you (e.g. *'Do have another helping of dessert'* or *'Go on: have a slice of delicious chocolate cake. I made it specially for you'*). It can seem hard to refuse such offers without being rude. However, it is possible to be polite and at the same time firm in sticking to what you want to do. If you are particularly plagued by others trying to force you to eat, you might find it helpful to rehearse two or three phrases so that they're on the tip of your tongue when you need them. Here are a few to get you started; below is space for you to add any more you come up with.

'No, thank you. It was delicious but I couldn't manage any more.'

'No, thank you. I won't have anything because I have just eaten.'

'No, thank you. I'll be eating later and I don't want to spoil my appetite.'

_____

_____

_____

_____

8 *Finally, take each moment of the day separately.*

We have already seen how important this is. It is very common for people to say to themselves: *'Well, I got that one wrong, so I might as well abandon any attempt to eat normally for the rest of the day.'* Instead, if something goes wrong, go back to your plan and see what it is that you are supposed to do next. If you can get back on to your plan immediately and stick to it for the rest of the day, then you can be confident that you have made real progress.

Devising strategies to suit yourself

The best way to put together a pack of techniques to prevent yourself running into difficulties, or to extricate yourself from dangerous situations, is to work out what will suit you best, and meet your particular needs most closely. You can do this by examining your monitoring sheets. This will show you:

- what situations are particularly difficult for you;

- what the circumstances are in which you are most likely to lose control and binge;

- what tactics you find most helpful in avoiding or coping with these situations and circumstances.

The key thing is to be one step ahead of trouble.

It is likely that, after a week or two of monitoring, certain patterns will become clear to you as you go over your monitoring sheets. You may find that you invariably binge after particular events, such as going shopping, or in particular circumstances, such as being on your own with no particular plans or appointments. Once you have realized this, you will be able to see in advance when you are likely to run into difficulty and to adapt arrangements to make things easier for you.

Below is an example of a situation identified as difficult and a way of dealing with it that can be planned in advance. Try to think of two or three other situations or circumstances that your monitoring sheets suggest are dangerous for you, and then to think of what you could do to head off the danger, and write them down in the space left below the example.

Difficult situation: Unpacking the shopping, which always leads on to a binge.

Action to head off the danger: Invite a friend in for a cup of tea while unpacking the shopping.

Difficult situation:

_____

Action to head off the danger:

_____

_____

Difficult situation:

_____

Action to head off the danger:

_____

_____

Difficult situation:

_____

Action to head off the danger:

_____

_____

Be sensible with alcohol

Many people find that their eating is particularly difficult to control after they have been drinking, because alcohol tends to undermine the resolve to control eating. It will be quite clear from your monitoring sheets whether this is the case for you. If it is, the solution is a simple one: *either drink in moderation or, if this is difficult for you, do not drink at all.*

You should be very strict about this while your prime goal is to restore order to your eating habits. Once you are no longer binge-eating and are confident of your control, you can take another look at your alcohol intake and decide when and how much it would be safe to drink. It must be stressed that *if you drink excessively you will not be able to make full use of this programme and it is unlikely that you will be able to overcome your problems with eating.*

Intervening in the moment

The section above on 'planning ahead' has set out some ideas for how you can arrange things in advance to make it easier to keep to your eating plan. However, *it is just as important to have plans prepared for what you will do when things go wrong.*

For example, you may well have an urge to eat when you come in from work. *It is very useful to have a list of things you could do instead of eating* (like going for a walk, having a bath, telephoning a friend, etc.); if you do, when you feel an urge to eat you can then start working your way through the list until the urge has passed.

It is common for people to say: *'If I have a strong urge to binge, however long I postpone it, in the end I will succumb.'* They feel that it is almost as if the binge has a will of its own, that it is lurking, and that in the end it will get them. In fact, if you do intervene and prevent a binge, the urge to eat does pass; and, of course, it is soon time for a planned meal or snack when eating is quite legitimate.

Intervening in this way is not easy. At first it might even seem impossible. But you can be reassured that *each time you do intervene successfully you make intervening in the future that much easier*. And the more often you intervene successfully, the less often the urge to binge will arise.

Your list of things to do in order to overcome the urge to binge and delay eating until the next meal or snack can include any activity which you feel might help, but in order to make sure you choose things that will be effective, it's worth considering the following guidelines :

- The activities you choose should be easy to do at times when you might feel an urge to eat – so, for example, in the winter when it may be dark and cold when you get in from work, going for a walk in the park may be neither pleasant nor safe.

- Activities which involve using your hands can be particularly helpful, e.g. knitting, sewing, handiwork, gardening, playing a musical instrument, etc. More passive activities, such as watching television, or activities which require mental concentration, such as reading a book, are unlikely to be effective in blocking out thoughts of food.

- Activities which remove you from your habitual eating places, like the kitchen, are often useful in emergencies. These would include outdoor activities such as going for a walk or a bicycle ride, but might also include things you can do indoors, like clearing out a cupboard or rearranging your CD shelves.

- Many people regard eating on some level as a treat or indulgence, so it is a good idea to include in your list some other activities you regard as self-indulgent, such as going to see a film in the afternoon, buying yourself a new item of clothing or a bunch of flowers, or telephoning a friend you seldom see. Often something as simple as a long hot bath using scented bath oil can make you feel better about yourself.

- Don't include on your list activities which you actually dislike. It is very important that your distracting activities are not tasks or duties which you will not actually want to do. So it is generally not advisable to include things like scrubbing the kitchen floor or going for a long run, unless you actually enjoy doing these things. A sense of virtuous achievement is not what you are aiming for here; rather, you are looking for a way to see yourself through a difficult period until it is a scheduled time for you to eat again.

The list you do make can obviously be added to or subtracted from as you try out the various activities and get an idea of how effective they are in different situations. It is a good idea to carry the list with you, so that when you feel an urge to eat you can immediately consult it and decide which of the activities you might use in that particular circumstance to tide you over until the next meal or snack time.

The two pages that follow are provided for you to write in your list. Use the first page to write in a provisional list; you should amend this as you gain experience of what does and does not work for you. Once you are confident of what the most effective activities are, write them down on the second page as your updated list. You can always update the list again if you discover anything particularly effective later. (Some spare pages are provided at the end of this workbook for you do to this.)

Provisional list of activities to fend off the urge to eat

Updated list of activities to fend off the urge to eat

_____

_____

_____

_____

_____

_____

_____

_____

_____

_____

_____

_____

_____

_____

_____

_____

_____

_____

_____

Before you move on

Before moving on to the next step of the course in Part Three, ask yourself the following questions:

---

*Have I been avoiding, wherever possible, those situations which
I have identified as ones in which I am likely to binge?*   YES / NO

---

*Have I regularly been planning ahead in an effort to be
'one step ahead of trouble'?*   YES / NO

---

*When things have gone wrong and I have been on the verge
of a binge, have I been attempting to intervene?*   YES / NO

---

*Have I been systematically working through a list of activities
in an effort to delay and prevent binge-eating?*   YES / NO

---

*Have I been able on some occasions to prevent a binge from
happening, either by careful planning or by actively intervening?*   YES / NO

If you can answer *'yes'* to all these questions, you should move on to the next step of the course in Part Three. If you cannot answer *'yes'* to all the questions, you should re-read this section and try again to follow all the guidelines it contains.

Extra Charts and Worksheets

Monitoring Sheet   Date: _____   Day: _____

Time	Food and liquid consumed	Place	B	C	Events/feelings

Monitoring Sheet

Date: _____ Day: _____

Time	Food and liquid consumed	Place	B	C	Events/feelings

Monitoring Sheet

Date: _____   Day: _____

Time	Food and liquid consumed	Place	B	C	Events/feelings

Monitoring Sheet   Date: _____   Day: _____

Time	Food and liquid consumed	Place	B	C	Events/feelings

Monitoring Sheet

Date: _____ Day: _____

Time	Food and liquid consumed	Place	B	C	Events/feelings

Time	Food and liquid consumed	Place	B	C	Events/feelings

Monitoring Sheet   Date: _____   Day: _____

Monitoring Sheet   Date: _____   Day: _____

Time	Food and liquid consumed	Place	B	C	Events/feelings

Review of this week's monitoring

Week from_____to_____

What are the particular times when binges seem more likely to occur?

_____

_____

What are the particular situations which tend to trigger binges?

_____

_____

Are there times when eating is relatively easy to control?

_____

_____

What types of food have you been eating during binges?

_____

_____

Are these foods different from the types you eat at other times, and if so how?

_____

_____

Are there long periods of time when you eat nothing at all?   YES / NO

How many times this week has a period of eating nothing
at all been followed by a binge?   _____

How many times this week has a day of strict dieting been
followed by a day when you binge?   _____

Any other observations

_____

_____

Review of this week's monitoring

Week from_____to_____

What are the particular times when binges seem more likely to occur?

_____

_____

What are the particular situations which tend to trigger binges?

_____

_____

Are there times when eating is relatively easy to control?

_____

_____

What types of food have you been eating during binges?

_____

_____

Are these foods different from the types you eat at other times, and if so how?

_____

_____

Are there long periods of time when you eat nothing at all?　　　　YES / NO

How many times this week has a period of eating nothing
at all been followed by a binge?

How many times this week has a day of strict dieting been
followed by a day when you binge?

Any other observations

_____

_____

Review of this week's monitoring

Week from_____to_____

What are the particular times when binges seem more likely to occur?

_____

_____

What are the particular situations which tend to trigger binges?

_____

_____

Are there times when eating is relatively easy to control?

_____

_____

What types of food have you been eating during binges?

_____

_____

Are these foods different from the types you eat at other times, and if so how?

_____

_____

Are there long periods of time when you eat nothing at all?   YES / NO

How many times this week has a period of eating nothing
at all been followed by a binge?   _____

How many times this week has a day of strict dieting been
followed by a day when you binge?   _____

Any other observations

_____

_____

Review of this week's monitoring

Week from_____to_____

What are the particular times when binges seem more likely to occur?

_____

_____

What are the particular situations which tend to trigger binges?

_____

_____

Are there times when eating is relatively easy to control?

_____

_____

What types of food have you been eating during binges?

_____

_____

Are these foods different from the types you eat at other times, and if so how?

_____

_____

Are there long periods of time when you eat nothing at all?   YES / NO

How many times this week has a period of eating nothing
at all been followed by a binge?   _____

How many times this week has a day of strict dieting been
followed by a day when you binge?   _____

Any other observations

_____

_____

Meal plan for weekdays/weekends/school holidays/other_____

_____ a.m.	Breakfast
_____ a.m.	Snack
_____ p.m.	Lunch
_____ p.m.	Snack
_____ p.m.	Supper
_____ p.m.	Snack

Meal plan for weekdays/weekends/school holidays/other_____

_____ a.m.	Breakfast
_____ a.m.	Snack
_____ p.m.	Lunch
_____ p.m.	Snack
_____ p.m.	Supper
_____ p.m.	Snack

Meal plan for weekdays/weekends/school holidays/other_____

_____ a.m.	Breakfast
_____ a.m.	Snack
_____ p.m.	Lunch
_____ p.m.	Snack
_____ p.m.	Supper
_____ p.m.	Snack

Meal plan for weekdays/weekends/school holidays/other_____

_____ a.m.	Breakfast
_____ a.m.	Snack
_____ p.m.	Lunch
_____ p.m.	Snack
_____ p.m.	Supper
_____ p.m.	Snack

Meal plan for weekdays/weekends/school holidays/other_____

_____ a.m.	Breakfast
_____ a.m.	Snack
_____ p.m.	Lunch
_____ p.m.	Snack
_____ p.m.	Supper
_____ p.m.	Snack

Meal plan for weekdays/weekends/school holidays/other_____

_____ a.m.	Breakfast
_____ a.m.	Snack
_____ p.m.	Lunch
_____ p.m.	Snack
_____ p.m.	Supper
_____ p.m.	Snack

Meal plan for weekdays/weekends/school holidays/other_____

_____ a.m.   Breakfast

_____ a.m.   Snack

_____ p.m.   Lunch

_____ p.m.   Snack

_____ p.m.   Supper

_____ p.m.   Snack

Meal plan for weekdays/weekends/school holidays/other_____

_____ a.m.   Breakfast

_____ a.m.   Snack

_____ p.m.   Lunch

_____ p.m.   Snack

_____ p.m.   Supper

_____ p.m.   Snack

Meal plan for weekdays/weekends/school holidays/other_____

_____ a.m.   Breakfast

_____ a.m.   Snack

_____ p.m.   Lunch

_____ p.m.   Snack

_____ p.m.   Supper

_____ p.m.   Snack

Monitoring sheet with meal plan

Meal Plan

Date:

Day:

——— a.m.	Breakfast	——— p.m.	Snack
——— a.m.	Snack	——— p.m.	Supper
——— p.m.	Lunch	——— p.m.	Snack

Time	Food and liquid consumed	Place	B	C	Events/feelings

Monitoring sheet with meal plan

Meal Plan　　**Date:**　　　　**Day:**

____ a.m.	Breakfast	____ p.m.	Snack
____ a.m.	Snack	____ p.m.	Supper
____ p.m.	Lunch	____ p.m.	Snack

Time	Food and liquid consumed	Place	B	C	Events/feelings

Monitoring sheet with meal plan

Meal Plan   **Date:**   **Day:**

____ a.m.	Breakfast	____ p.m.	Snack
____ a.m.	Snack	____ p.m.	Supper
____ p.m.	Lunch	____ p.m.	Snack

Time	Food and liquid consumed	Place	B	C	Events/feelings

Monitoring sheet with meal plan

Meal Plan　　**Date:**　　**Day:**

——— a.m.　Breakfast　　——— p.m.　Snack

——— a.m.　Snack　　——— p.m.　Supper

——— p.m.　Lunch　　——— p.m.　Snack

Time	Food and liquid consumed	Place	B	C	Events/feelings

70

Monitoring sheet with meal plan

Meal Plan   **Date:**   **Day:**

a.m.	Breakfast	p.m.	Snack
a.m.	Snack	p.m.	Supper
p.m.	Lunch	p.m.	Snack

Time	Food and liquid consumed	Place	B	C	Events/feelings

Monitoring sheet with meal plan

Meal Plan **Date:** **Day:**

_____ a.m. Breakfast _____ p.m. Snack

_____ a.m. Snack _____ p.m. Supper

_____ p.m. Lunch _____ p.m. Snack

Time	Food and liquid consumed	Place	B	C	Events/feelings

Monitoring sheet with meal plan

Meal Plan **Date:** **Day:**

_____ a.m. Breakfast _____ p.m. Snack

_____ a.m. Snack _____ p.m. Supper

_____ p.m. Lunch _____ p.m. Snack

Time	Food and liquid consumed	Place	B	C	Events/feelings

Monitoring sheet with meal plan

Meal Plan

Date: _____

Day: _____

_____ a.m.	Breakfast
_____ a.m.	Snack
_____ p.m.	Lunch
_____ p.m.	Snack
_____ p.m.	Supper
_____ p.m.	Snack

Time	Food and liquid consumed	Place	B	C	Events/feelings

Monitoring sheet with meal plan

Meal Plan   **Date:**   **Day:**

——— a.m.	Breakfast
——— a.m.	Snack
——— p.m.	Lunch
——— p.m.	Snack
——— p.m.	Supper
——— p.m.	Snack

Time	Food and liquid consumed	Place	B	C	Events/feelings

Updated list of activities to fend off the urge to eat

Updated list of activities to fend off the urge to eat

Updated list of activities to fend off the urge to eat

Updated list of activities to fend off the urge to eat

Updated list of activities to fend off the urge to eat

Thoughts and Reflections

Thoughts and Reflections

Thoughts and Reflections

Thoughts and Reflections

Thoughts and Reflections

Thoughts and Reflections

86

Thoughts and Reflections